POWERPOINT® REALITY
Slides in Real Time for Real Audiences With Real Easy Steps

J. Kanan Sawyer, Ph.D.
West Chester University

Allyn & Bacon

Boston Columbus Indianapolis New York San Francisco Upper Saddle River Amsterdam Cape Town Dubai

London Madrid Milan Munich Paris Montreal Toronto Delhi

Mexico City Sao Paulo Sydney Hong Kong Seoul Singapore Taipei Tokyo

Editor in Chief/Acquisitions Editor: Karon Bowers
Editorial Assistant: Megan Sweeney
Associate Managing Editor: Bayani Mendoza de Leon
Manufacturing Buyer: Mary Ann Gloriande
Marketing Manager: Blair Tuckman
Art Director: Nancy Wells
Cover Designer: Candace Rowley
Cover Image: mcswin / iStockphoto

Allyn & Bacon
is an imprint of

www.pearsonhighered.com

2 16

ISBN-13: 978-0-205-00038-8
ISBN-10: 0-205-00038-X

TABLE OF CONTENTS

A DIFFERENT LENS

IN THE BOOK/ NOT IN THE BOOK/ WHY THIS BOOK?...

As you may have guessed, not every speech needs visual support, and those speeches that do may not need PowerPoint™ support. If your speech does not, well, you shouldn't have purchased this book and shouldn't go through this process. However, if you do need visual support for your talk, PowerPoint slides can be an amazing way to help your audience visually picture (redundant, right?) what you have to say.

PowerPoint slides are an incredible tool for showing visual information to a large audience, helping to guide an audience along the structure of a speech, adding visual movement to a talk, helping your audience to follow and recall your ideas, and even professionally presenting small amounts of text.

If you have chosen to use slides – let's not fall into the trap of creating slides that make our audience cringe. Sadly, most slides do. With so many PowerPoint help guides on the market, why is it that we are still seeing… this?!?!!? ⟶

Marketability for Career success

- Skills & Experience gained
  - Confidence Building is crucial to showing socials skills in networking
  - Team Building will become a neccesary part of any job or project
  - Building Character will help to make you a more marketable property
  - Time Management Skills will open up more options for you
  - Be both Honest & Responsible

Good question. I have used any number of PowerPoint textbooks in my career and, as a professor, I have assigned any number of them to my students. What I found myself doing was supplementing these books with some very foundational information – from a *communication theory* perspective. EEK. Before you put this book down because in the first page it used the word "theory," consider instead that what you heard was this:

PowerPoint presentations are failing because they have missed the mark of effectively *communicating* with their audiences.

There is an entire discipline of Communication Studies that has grown since Greek times and instructs its followers that messages must be centered on the "audience" in order to have an impact. If messages are distracting or disconnected, well, then you can kiss your impact goodbye. So, where is the connection with PowerPoint???

It seems that most PowerPoint books fall into two categories: 1) "How To" do everything books, and 2) design books. This book is a little of both but also what you will find here is a look at PowerPoint through a different lens – as a means to link your audience to you and vice versa. You will hear the word <u>audience</u> **a lot** throughout this text.

MAKING IT EASY .

It is rare that I speak to a group that has no PowerPoint experience (if that is you, don't panic, we can get you through). Some folks have started with mandatory PowerPoint assignments in *elementary* school! Most people have had to put together a presentation for something or another… and everyone seems to have seen a slide show.

So, if you have no experience in opening a slide or putting text on a slide then you may should know that you may need a "How To" manual or an online tutorial at some point to learn the basics (consider: http://www.actden.com/pp2007/index.htm - it's like the Dick and Jane of tutorials). If, however, you have those two criteria down – or feel comfortable doing a quick internet search (e.g., "insert text in PowerPoint") – then you have the skill set to make this book a valuable tool, which will provide you with the following:

-    a simple means of connecting you to your audience
-    step by step instructions for creating <u>audience-centered</u> templates
-    tools for altering images *without* the need of other software
-    a clear understanding of how slides work *with* your speech
-    comfortable delivery techniques that will differentiate you from other presenters
-    and (of course) a few tricks

My goal is to provide you with steps in a simple format that will eliminate anxiety and keep PowerPoint from being a big time-suck in your life. While the images in this book are specific to PC users, the design concepts apply to MAC users, as do many of the short cuts, which are in both "languages."

Sound good? (And, now that "theory" word is a bit less jarring.)

CRITICS, OPPONENTS, DETRACTORS – WHAT'S UP WITH THAT?

Before we launch into making your life easier when working with PowerPoint, we need to take a quick moment to address the common criticisms of the medium so that you will not fall into these traps.

If you have seen a PowerPoint show then you have probably seen at least some bad PowerPoint. In fact, one author even claims not only that PowerPoint is evil, but that, "*Power corrupts. PowerPoint corrupts absolutely*" (tee hee hee) (This is from Edward Tufte's, 2003 article in Wired Magazine, in case you're looking!)

The arguments against PowerPoint contend that slides:
-    have poor visual quality
-    limit content
-    disconnect speakers and audiences

Marketability for Career success

- Skills & Experience gained
  - Confidence Building is crucial to showing socials skills in networking
  - Team Building will become a neccesary part of any job or project
  - Building Character will help to make you a more marketable property
  - Time Management Skills will open up more options for you
- Be both Honest & Responsible

Yup. Totally right. No argument here. Ah… but this is because PowerPoint is being used in a way that does all of these things. If we redesign our slides, use them as *aids* to talks rather than to be the talk itself, and don't use them when they distract or are not necessary,… then we can agree with the critics and still be effective. Let's do that!

How? Like this…

You'll note that the arrangement of this book starts with a section on *Audience*, which is followed by an *Organizing* section containing discussions of both text and images (typically the bulk of "how-to" manuscripts), and lastly, some *Adding* and *Presenting*. As you read along, your attention will be shifted from what you can do with PowerPoint to what you ought to do in order to connect and change your audiences. The result will be a presentation unlike that of any of your colleagues. Your presentation will be remembered because your audience will finally know that you are talking *to them*!

So, what you get here is a bit different. This book is an attempt to shift your focus. It is an attempt to help you *connect* to your audience. Read on… and you will find yourself having a few "Ah Ha!" and "Reeeealllly???!" moments that change your PowerPoint slides (and your presentations) forever.

Enjoy.

AUDIENCE

"TO... NOT FROM"

Why is *audience* the thing that most PowerPoint books have failed to address? Communication scholars will tell you that this is the foundation of our public address. Yet suddenly it's all about us? Where is the "audience" in PowerPoint?

For example, who is the audience for *this* (actual slide)?!?!

If you were on the receiving end of this slide show presentation, would you be captivated? Engaged? Appreciative of how your speaker knew you – or took the time to target the speech just to you? Probably not. More likely, you would be thinking... "huh?"

Before we criticize, let us reflect on two important considerations. First, it is likely that each of us has constructed equally as dissociative slides. Second, audiences change. We may give the same speech of the same topic to several different groups and, yet, have constructed only one set of slides. Even more out of our control, many employees are at the mercy of their employers who use stock slide templates for <u>all</u> of their presentations.

Unfortunately, these have become our excuses. These are the pitfalls of *habitual slide creation*. Hearken back to the days of your college public speaking class (or, perhaps you are in such a class now or side stepped this all-important course). Your professor would have instructed you to make every speech be about, for, and to the very audience in front of you. Sure, the topic, format, and even much of your evidence may be the same, but if you did not relate your stories, examples, language, and style to your specific listeners, then you would have failed to meet a very basic communication principle. (Aristotle would be distraught!)

Speeches and slides must be "audience-centered." However, for as basic a foundation as this may sound, consider the slide right here. *Who* is the audience?

Is it for mothers-to-be, hospital care workers, or nursing students? Is it a little disconnected?

GOOD PRENATAL CARE IS..

• NO CIGARETTE SMOKING

• NO ALCOHOL AND DRUG USE

• LOW EXPOSURE TO TERATOGENS

• AVOID EXCESSIVE PHYSICAL WORK

Let's fix it!!

This new version of the same information helps to clarify our all-important audience! See?? The information is the same. The speaker is the same. Yet the visual elements are very easily manipulated to be about a *specific* audience. In this case, the audience is the King County Prenatal Care System and the speaker is the company Nurses Training, Inc.

The images and the layout can be grabbed right off the audience's website! (Read on for laws from the Fair Use Act on image grabbing as well as text versus visual focus!)

Some readers, at this point, will be panicked. Every audience?!? Every speech?! Who has the time? This is where template construction is your friend.

TEMPLATE CONSTRUCTION

Templates are not backgrounds. Backgrounds are the colors behind your words or visuals. Templates are the designs that make up the tone, format (or organization), and layout of your entire PowerPoint show.

Microsoft offers you several templates or "Design Themes" along with their software.

Some of these templates are as old as time. Office 2007 has updated many of the Microsoft designs to be more visually appealing than in previous versions. That's great – except for one thing. As good looking as they are… Microsoft still doesn't know who <u>your</u> audience is.

No matter how much you think that your slides are pretty or captivating (or even shocking!), **unaltered Microsoft PowerPoint templates will never be about or for your specific audience.**

There are two solutions:
- design your own templates
- manipulate given designs

AUDIENCE FEEL

Before you select which of the two options of template construction you will use, you must get a "feel" for your audience. The best way to do this is to simply look at the materials put out by your audience, which are designed for this very purpose – such as a company website. Websites are created by companies to be a visual representation of that organization's tenor and professionalism. Look at your own school or company's website. Compare that to its direct competitors. Do you get a different feel from each of them? Is one more friendly, inviting, playful, business-minded, modern, or old school?

While we you are looking at homepages, you may find that some websites' visual appeal is less than stellar. You may see clutter, poor images, overuse of text, too many types of fonts, or other issues that will violate many of the recommendations laid out in this manual. Remember, first, that visual aids have a different purpose (i.e., supporting a speech) than do websites, which are stand-alone mediums. Remember, second, you aren't supposed to copy… that's plagiarism. ☺ You need to understand, emote, and relate. You are supposed to have your audience upon first glance say, "Hey, that's about me!"
So, take a peek. Get a feel – and read on to determine your next step!

Note: If your group has no website, no worries. Look at brochures, letterhead, graphic designs, and sales materials – even office décor! Get a feel about your group from the materials that they send out as representations of who they are. Remember that if your group *does* have a website, they will update often and you should always be checking back for style and image changes.

LET'S TAKE A MOMENT TO DISCUSS LEGALITY.

Unless you designed the background or logo, unless you took the picture, unless you created the company-specific color (like Tiffany blue or Coca Cola red), then you must have _written permission to_ use these elements. If you do not, it's stealing! (Don't steal.)

It is difficult to find the details for penalties related to image poaching. Below is a brief overview (further details may be found many places, including: http://www.buscalegis.ufsc.br/revistas/index.php /buscalegis/article/viewFile/3450/3021, which is the source for some of this information):

The penalties for copying images, audio, or others' materials without permission include:
-   Fines up to the actual amount of damages
-   Statutory damages up to $100,000 *per* infringement
-   Criminal penalties of up to one year in jail and fines up to $25,000

You may notice that many of your professors do or have used others' images or logos. This is often (but not always) permitted under the protection of "fair use." Fair Use refers to the copyright standards that allow individuals to copy others' work for "purposes such as…

teaching, scholarship, or research…" without requiring author permission. That being said, the copyright guidelines further clarify that educators or those in an educational setting cannot just take what they want and use it. This means that "fair use" has limits, which is why even teachers are limited to 5 images per author and no more than 10% of a text or 1,000 words. If an educator violates this standard, "depending on the circumstances, educators may not be required to pay statutory damages (as high as $150,000 per instance), but they may still have to pay copyright owners actual damages caused by their *illegal* copying, plus legal fees."

Therefore, if you choose to use others' images, **you must pay for usage** as dictated by the author and be sure to cite: author's name, title of work – and it is from the internet, name of site, date posted and/ or revised, date obtained, and URL. If you select an image but drastically alter it such that it is "distinctly different from the original," your work would not be considered "poaching."

If your co-workers or friends are using the ole "copying what I wanna" method and are not covered under the Fair Use provisions or do not have written permission from the image or text owners then those folks (or you) are in fact breaking the law. If you use these elements in the classroom as part of learning, then you have permission to do so. If you, however, use these classroom created slides as part of a portfolio or as examples of your work that you show outside the classroom then you are NOT covered under Fair Use and you are subject to the full penalty of the law.

(Good to know, huh!?!)

TO CITE OR NOT TO CITE… SHOULD NEVER BE A QUESTION.

If you have developed a strong speech grounded on research, you want your audience to know! Speeches are a time to flaunt your credibility but putting together cumbersome references in a visual medium can create a quandary. To simply paste up a list of references in a final slide would violate many of our rules of text design (read on). Not to reference them at all would violate legal and ethical standards. The choice of how to cite your sources, however, is up to you. How should you reference your contributing sources without cluttering your slides??

First, consider again that PowerPoint is a visual medium. Blocks of text are better suited to handouts and your audience may indeed wish to have a take-home list of your sources. If so, present your sources in that medium.

Second, you may want your audience to see your sources as they come up in your talk and, thus, listing names on each slide per bullet could be the most clear communication method – just keep your text amount minimal.

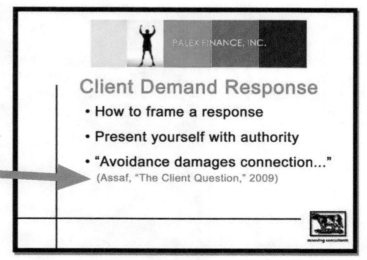

"3 out of 4 presentations, according to John Zagger of the New York Times, use distracting PowerPoint slides!"

Third, remember that your slides will aid a verbal presentation and simply stating your sources out loud is always the best way to "show" your credibility!

Whatever you decide, keep your references in sync with the look, feel, and good design rules of your PowerPoint slides – and remember that citations should be announced or visible for anything that you have taken from another source.

Charts

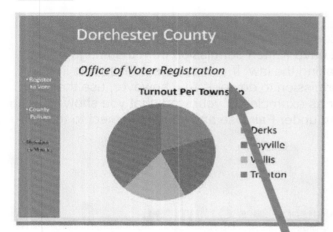 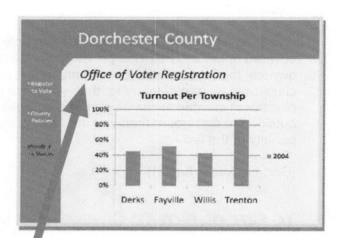

Cites

Images

Lynn Sawyer, Sawyer Photography 2010

DESIGN YOUR OWN TEMPLATES

Designing your own PowerPoint templates is far easier than you may have guessed. Those with lots of PowerPoint skill can get super fancy but even those with the most basic knowledge can design audience-centered templates that grab viewers!

Design is about shape and placement. Audience-centered templates are about color and tone. Once you have "researched" the look of your group, set up slides that demonstrate an understanding and keen attention to their tone, font, colors, and (with permission from your audience or under Fair Use guidelines) the layout.

For instance, if you were part of the "XMS Green Marketing" group and giving a talk to Kelson's Gourmet grocery, you would take a peek at Kelson's **current website...**

... and could create a show using any of the following four looks:

Note: Each template uses elements of the existing website but that four different looks are developed – each of which effectively links to the audience.

Look Number One

The first look (because we have permission of the audience!) literally mimics the look of the webpage – including images and layout. Next, it mimics the background color of the website and pastes a box of that color over the website text to create a space for new words! (If you cannot find the specific color in the PowerPoint "format background" standard colors, you can actually copy the webpage and crop down to create color boxes. (See the instructions later in this section).

The next two looks also clearly link to the audience by copying specific elements of the webpage.

Look Number Two

Look Two uses the same font type as well as the audience's logo and pictures with a very simple and basic background (removing elements can keep the audience feel but help to limit clutter on your slides).

Look Number Three

Look Three uses the logo and font type but mimics the background of some of the photos rather than using specific images!

Look Number Four

Look Four keeps it basic. For folks who are worried that excessive creativity is needed to connect to your audience, stop worrying!

This looks simply changes the colors on a Microsoft template and add the company logo. No frills– but still connects!

Time to Create??

So many options. So little time!
Yes, time. How (you may ask) difficult is this process and how much time will it take?

Those new to creating their own slides can be trepidacious about the effort involved in putting these together. Relax.

This guide is designed to make the steps easy – and we start in the very next section.

STEPS TO CREATING A SLIDE TEMPLATE

Step 1: Mimic Background Color or Copy Background Elements

Embrace your right click. Most slide elements can be copied (remember… with permission or under the Fair Use guidelines – this cannot be stressed enough!!!) by simply putting your cursor on the element that you desire to have on your slide, right clicking and copying – then pasting onto your slides. Easy!

> **MAC vs. PC Note:**
> Right click?! If you are a MAC person, you may be feeling left out at this notation and laughing that another computer guide has fallen prey to the swift grasp of the PC fad.
>
> Not to worry, in this text you will find shortcut methods in both PC and MAC language and, where they have been unwittingly omitted, remember that these steps are typically easy to find with a quick search on the internet!
>
> (ps… control click on a MAC is the same as right click on a PC) ☺

As you go about selecting and pasting, you will see that some elements will paste beautifully, some will come up in pieces (bummer – lots of right clicking) and if you want more than just a single element... lots and lots of right clicking. Watch out for carpal tunnel!

Alternatively, consider the use of "**Ctrl-Alt-PrtSc**" – or a "Print Screen" / Screen Capture copy method, which will capture whatever you are showing on your desktop. You can then paste the element onto your slide ("**Ctrl + V**") and crop out unwanted elements or paste over them. (MAC users can do the same function with "**Command-Control-Shift-3**," which also places the image onto your clipboard so it can then be pasted into a slide.)

For example, if you go to the Kelson website, select "Ctrl + Alt + Prt Sc," and then paste (right click or "Ctrl + V") it onto a blank slide, you will get:

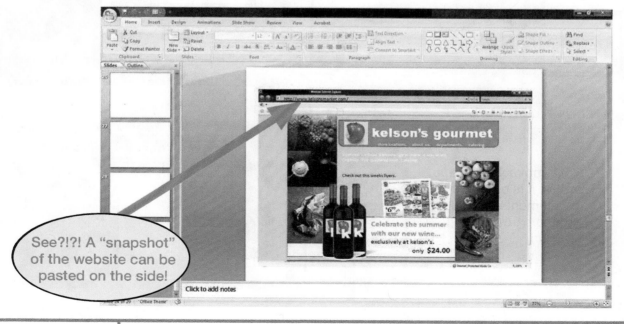

See?!?! A "snapshot" of the website can be pasted on the side!

Step 2: Add a Space for Text or Images

As you might note from the example above, some website "backgrounds" are not a suitable basis for layering on your text or images. This one is FULL of advertisements and excess images. If you tried to add your own stuff to this, the slide would be busy and cluttered.

In other instances, the background may be complex and make your text hard to see or be distracting to the eye. YOU NEED SPACE!!

How do you get that space? Add some boxes! It's that simple. Background color-matched boxes or other shapes placed on top of unnecessary elements will add areas on the slide for *your* words and images. It's like painting over the middle of a canvas.

Here's how:
1. Go to the "Insert" Tab and select your shape (in this case, it's a square but you may need a circle or some other shape to hide what you don't want & leave what you do).

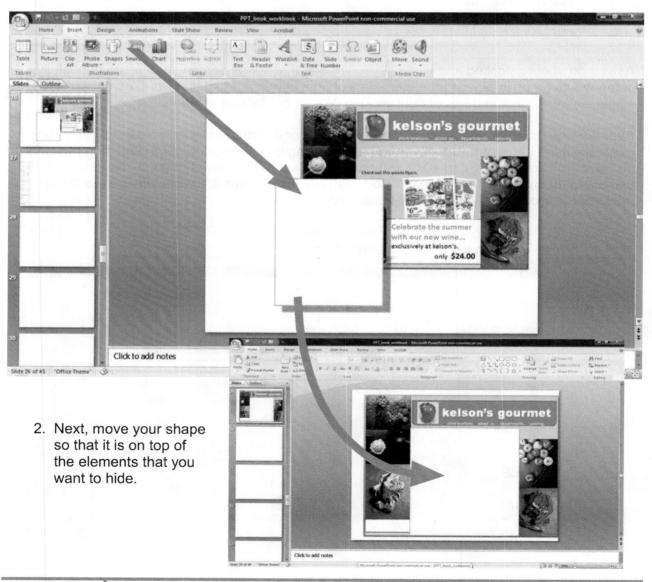

2. Next, move your shape so that it is on top of the elements that you want to hide.

3. Be sure to change the shape so that it matches the <u>background color</u> of your slide.

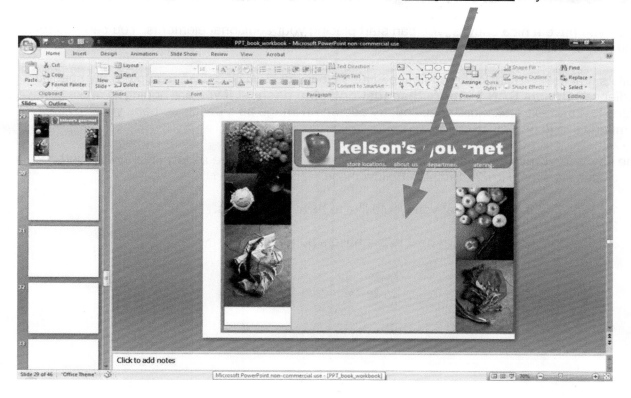

Now you have a clean canvas! If you would like even more room for your own information or images, just place another color-matched shape over more images until you get the perfect blend of room for you and look from them.

Creating That Perfect Color Match

Most colors are created by right clicking and selecting "format background." From this spot, you can alter from limitless possibilities. (MAC users can also select the shape and then open the Toolbox to the Formatting Palette and select "Colors, Weights, and Fills.")

However, what if you cannot find your chosen background color and your created colors just seem a bit off? Do not fret. Use your "Ctrl + Alt + Prt Sc" function again to copy the website and simply crop down to just a color section of your desired background color.

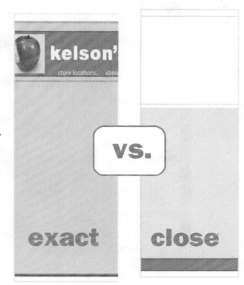

Next, you can make this box bigger or copy the one box and paste it EVERYWHERE that you want a blank spot! This is an automatic exact color match! (See the Visuals section to learn how to "Crop.")

Step 3: Layer With Key Images, Terms, Or Other "Template" Elements

Once you have a nice canvas, you can start placing your additional elements. You can add text, pictures, or even bullets that are specific to the audience.

Bullets that are specific to the audience? Huh? How can such little dashes capture my specific audience? **Bullets CAN be more than just dots and dashes!** If you are hoping to make your slides just that extra bit more specified, try adding an image as a bullet, perhaps your company's logo or a picture!?!

The key is to always make sure that these are large enough to see as tiny little bullets and do not clutter the slide. How?? Simple! Follow these steps:

1. Highlight the words that you would like to have with bullets.
2. Go to the "Home" Tab.
3. Click on the <u>arrow down</u> next to the bullets button.

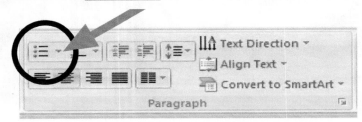

4. Select the "Bullets and Numbering" option.

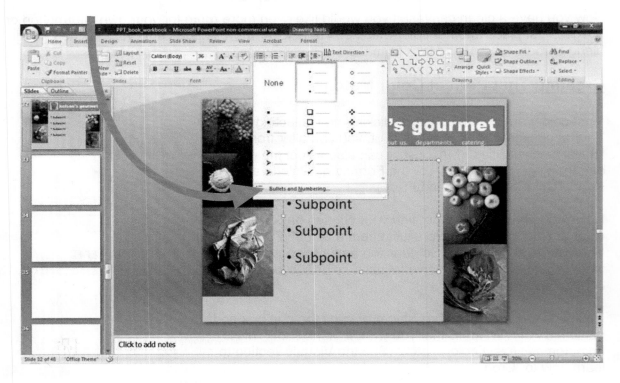

5. Select "Picture."

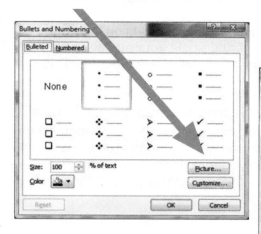

fyi: the "Pictures" you will see are stock images. ew... Most of these are pretty boring (e.g., a red box).

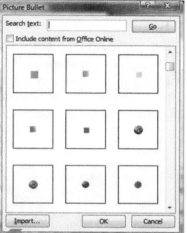

6. Click to "Import" and select from any image saved on your computer – including any images saved from internet searches or a homepage (remember image copyright! ☺).

7. Select "Add" – NOT "Add To" – and your image will appear as an option.

8. Click to add your option and it will appear!

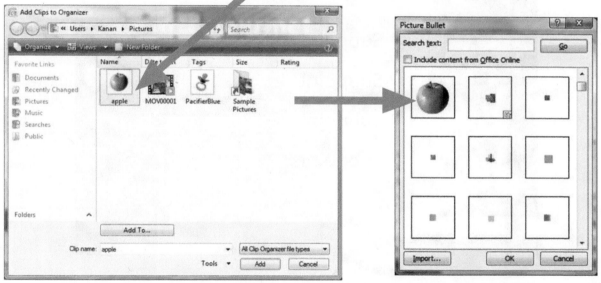

TRA LA!!!!

Your bullet will appear! If it is too **BIG** or too tiny, go back to the first screen and play with the image size with "size"/ % of text." Fun, huh!?!?! (And, totally audience-centered).

Step 4: Include an Author Identifying Element (as needed)

As you are wrapping up the final steps to creating your templates, you should consider one last element. You. Primary visual cues in your slides should be <u>of and about your audience</u> but this does not mean that those folks wouldn't benefit from a visual reminder of who *you* are. This can happen in a few ways.

First, you may decide to have your name on an initial slide. Second, you may choose to have it on all subsequent slides (e.g., *XMS Green Marketing*). Third, you may elect to have some visual element such as a logo from your group or company appear throughout the presentation. These elements are **_not_** necessary but can provide a link between you and "them." This also means that you do not need to ditch all aspects your company-designed templates (just change the focus).

Step 5: Add Your Content

OK. Templates are made. Now is the time that you add your content. Do not add content until your templates and verbal presentation are complete. This will keep you focused and your organization clear. As shown before, once you have both elements complete, finishing your slides is just a matter of placing your talk onto your templates.

After some pasting…finished!!! And this section included some tricky stuff!

(For guidelines about how much text you should include, image placement, and even what kind of text/ font to use – read on to Organization and Adding!)

MANIPULATE GIVEN DESIGNS

You may not be a whiz at creating PowerPoint elements or you just may not want to go through the process. You may have a stock presentation that every person in your company must use with every single client. Again, no worries. A few minor adjustments or additions to your stock templates or Microsoft "Design Themes" can still link you to your audience.

Design Themes are found in the "Design" Tab and show little pictures of *looks* for your slides.

MAC users will want to use the tabs shown above each slide and select "Slide Themes."

Step 1: Select a Theme that Best Matches Your Audience.

Yes, this is still important! (In fact, it's the point). Go through each of the looks and see what has a layout or even coloring that seems to best fit your audience. These don't have to be perfect – how could they be? – but you want to start with the design that asks the least amount of work from you.

Remember these?

Select the one with the best fit!

Step 2: Alter Colors and Layer to Clarify Audience Link

Again … those Microsoft folks don't know your audience. None of these themes will have a direct link to the group with whom *you* are speaking. Now is the time for some simple alterations.

Decide what basic changes will help to best create visual links to your audience. Will it be a change of background color? Do you need to alter the font of the text? Could you realign the text from left justified to centered – or vice versa?

Any other these elements can be used to mimic the feel and/ or tone of your audience. None should take more than a few seconds but do make sure to give yourself enough time to play with color choices (see below).

For example, consider this Design Theme with two different looks (all created by only changes of color, font, or adding a circle!)

One Theme/ Two Manipulations

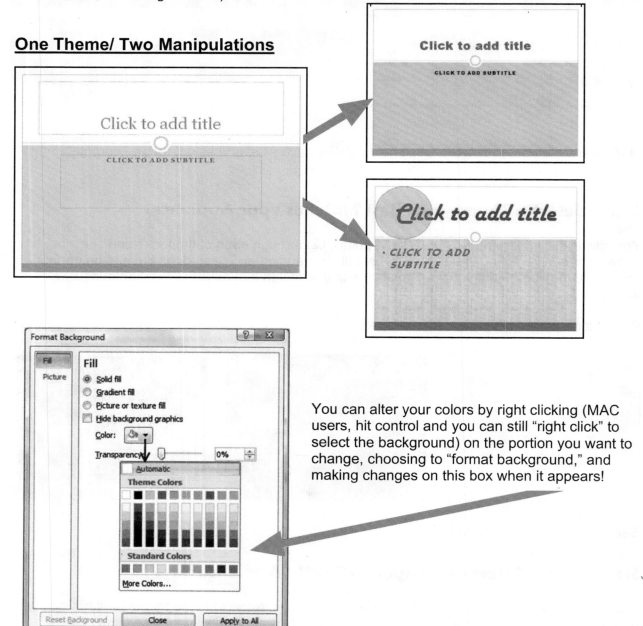

You can alter your colors by right clicking (MAC users, hit control and you can still "right click" to select the background) on the portion you want to change, choosing to "format background," and making changes on this box when it appears!

Just like above, once you have a nice canvas, you can start adding additional elements. Using the example shown earlier, you can see how simple manipulation serves as the foundation for your slide and the next steps help to complete it.

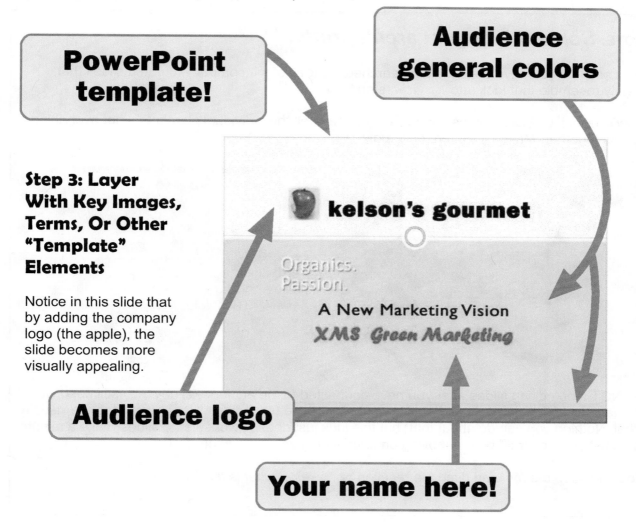

PowerPoint template!

Audience general colors

Step 3: Layer With Key Images, Terms, Or Other "Template" Elements

Notice in this slide that by adding the company logo (the apple), the slide becomes more visually appealing.

Audience logo

kelson's gourmet

Organics.
Passion.

A New Marketing Vision
XMS Green Marketing

Your name here!

Step 4: Include an Author Identifying Element (as needed)

You may not feel the need for your name or your company name on your slides but if you do decide to include it, be sure that it is easy to read and added in a spot that does not clash with the look or layout of your other slide elements.

You may simply include your name on the first slide (part of your introduction or as a backdrop to your talk as you begin) or can include your name on all slides. Be sure that you name or company name does not overshadow the focus on your audience!

Step 5: Add Your Content...

Follow the steps from the coming sections of this text to complete the look of your slides and to finalize your visual presentation!

NOTE: *Some things just aren't pretty.*

Let's say that you have done it all (researched the look of the company, created slides that clearly resemble that look, etc...). Now, step back.

How does it look? Sometimes even when you have all the individual elements – not everything comes together. Maybe it's even, er, ...ugly.

 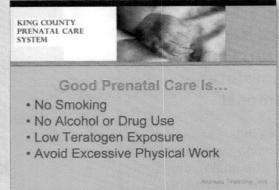

Do NOT stop editing slides after you have connected to the audience. They may still need work. Perhaps all of the elements looked fine on their website (or... didn't. Not all websites are visually ideal. Nothing you can do about that) but this look just doesn't work on the slides. Take a minute to adjust your "overall" before moving on to changing colors or deleting elements.

You can keep the *feel* and ditch the reaction of, *"yikes... what is that!?"*

Repeated Use Templates

Company Slides

If your boss insists that you use company templates, you may have little control over what elements cannot be removed from your slides. You can, however, still focus on the overall look and appeal of the slide.

Standard corporate templates can be modified in the very same way that basic Microsoft templates can be altered. Add images, change colors, include audience logos, and show that as much as you are advertising yourself, you are all about them!

Company Template

Linked to Audience

The Same Audience Over and Over Again

Another issue with slide templates is showing one audience the same templates over and over again. As important as it is to be consistent, it is just as important to let your audience know that your presentation was prepared just for them… and just for this talk! If you have had (or been) that teacher who is still using the same transparencies from 1971 – or the same slides since the 1980s (yeah… did you know that PowerPoint has been around for 20 years?!) then you know that slides can disconnect you from your audience just by appearing tired or overused.

There is no one template for a particular audience. To be effective, you need only to show a visual connection – but those visual elements can change per talk. For instance:

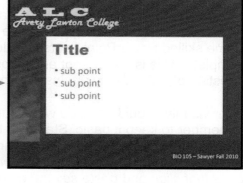

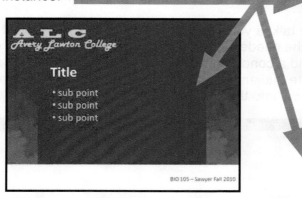

Avoid drastic changes for every talk (these are REALLY basic ☺). It is important not to appear to be scattered!

Now that your templates are complete, they can be used as the building blocks to <u>organizing</u> your audience-centered slides!

ORGANIZATION

OUTLINES

Nothing is worse than a speaker who exclaims, "But, I spent forever on my slides!" Uh oh. Bad choice. Spend forever on your *speech* and your slides will naturally reveal themselves (really!). All you will need to do is create visuals that can help your audience to: 1) **follow** your presentation and 2) **recall** your presentation.

How does one make slides soooo easily? Look to the outline of your speech.

SPEECH TO VISUAL AID LINK

Slides are like speeches. They have an introduction, a body, and a conclusion. These elements should match your verbal presentation; after all, the visuals only <u>aid your talk</u>. Aristotle would recommend that you think about your logos (that's a fancy old Greek word for *arguments*). Do! Use the outline that you have already put together for your speech to direct the text (don't just cut and paste your outline; you'll need to edit first) and select images for your slides as a means of "showing" your arguments. (hint hint… you should put together your speech *first*).

HOW MANY SLIDES???

There is no magic number on how many slides you should have per minute. Speakers often want to know… "how many slides are required?" Sorry. There is no precise answer to this. Some skilled PowerPoint users can do in two slides what may take others thirty-two to complete. This is a matter of animation use and creative layouts. Don't get caught up in the question of, "how many?" – instead think about what in your talk needs visual support.

Your visuals should coincide with your talk. If you are struggling to make your verbal… visual, remember to keep it basic. Start with the needed elements: an intro slide, a preview slide, one slide per main point, a review slide, and a conclusion slide. Add slides for subpoints as needed. Begin your construction by creating one audience-centered slide (as described above) and then *copy that slide* and *paste several of them* into the presentation.

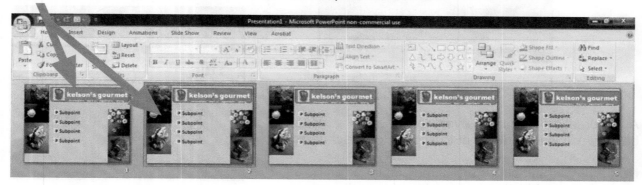

(Don't re-create it time and time again! Recreations can cause "bouncing" or slight shifts in location when shown that make the words and images appear to "bounce" up and down.)

Next, alter the slides so that they clearly link to the outline. Here's how that would look *per slide*:

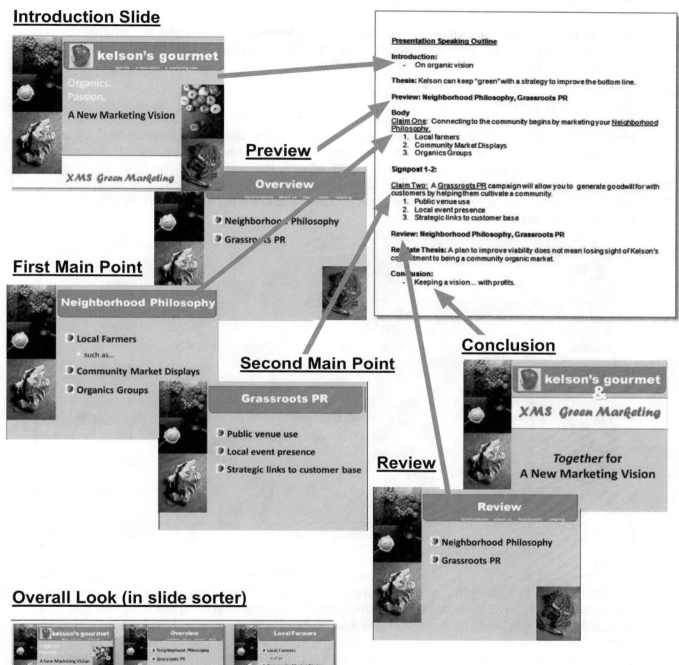

Introduction Slide

Preview

First Main Point

Second Main Point

Conclusion

Review

Overall Look (in slide sorter)

Go to the **Texting Section** below for guidelines on font size, type, and number of words. Go to the **Images Section** to determine how to follow the logos/organization of your speech outline if you choose not to use or to limit your text.

COMMON VISUAL OUTLINING ERRORS

While matching your slides to your outline, it is important to be aware of a few common visual outlining errors that can lead your audience astray. Hopefully, you have heard many of these before but will heed an additional word of caution.

EEK... MISLEADING HEADINGS

Headers (or slide titles) should match your agenda/preview slide. Creating headers by using subpoints or details is like telling your audience, "In the next few minutes, we will talk about "A, B, C" and then proceeding to talk about " h, #3, iii". It is the writing equivalent of creating a Table of Contents with one set of terms but inside the book having each chapter title be something totally different. How would you know what chapter you were in? It's even more difficult when the audience can't flip back.

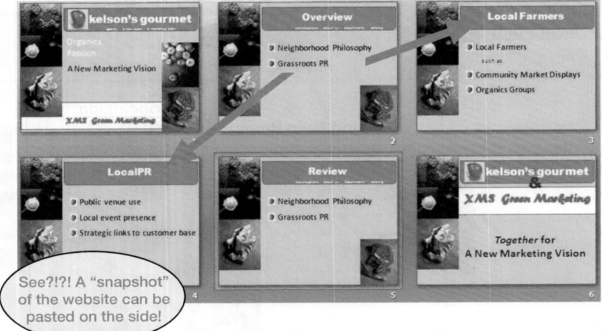

See?!?! A "snapshot" of the website can be pasted on the side!

While you may know where you are and what's up, your listeners are going through a complete mental exercise. You are insisting that they not tune out for a second and that they have committed to memory the outline of your speech so that you can elaborate on the details and they won't be lost as to where you are. AUDIENCES GET LOST. Help them out. Always make sure that the only headers that you use are the exact same words that you verbally/ visually previewed (e.g., see the presentation on page 25. Notice how all the headers are pulled off Slide #2 – word for word).

EEK... THE FIRST SLIDE GIVES IT AWAY

The first slide of your presentation *should* pull the audience into your talk. However, too many speakers will put the end of their talk (the "ask" or the conclusion) on that initial slide – allowing audiences to tune out or create barriers. This is especially problematic if your presentation is persuasive in any way.

If your first slide to a group of nurses for a presentation about how to discuss nutrition with pregnant women states, "Unhealthy Babies: You MUST Tell Your Patients To Eat Right!" – you might be in trouble. You have not yet convinced your audience of either the problems or your particular solution…. Eek! Your audience will begin creating all sorts of counter arguments or alternative choices in their heads from the start.

NO

EEK... NEGLECTING THE NEED FOR A THEME

Have you ever entered someone's house and knew that the entire thing was decorated out of Pottery Barn? Or IKEA? This is a theme. It is a look. However, what happens when you walk into one room and see IKEA, the next room screams Shabby Chic, and the next is early fraternity throw back? Things just seem off. This happens far too often in PowerPoint.

Instead, remember to link to your *verbal introduction* with the first visual slide. If you plan to begin talking about how nurses have vital conversations with their patients and then give an example of one woman that you talked to…

…then a revised slide might read, "Unhealthy Babies? What Should We Discuss With Our Patients?" This type of title grabs but doesn't give it all away!

Better!

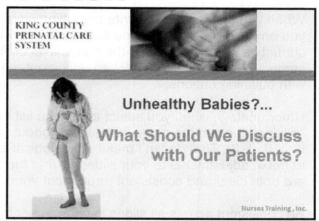

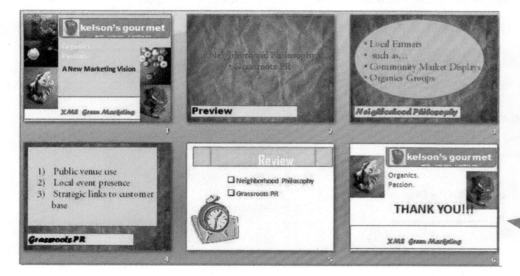

Lack of theme is typically an issue of changing looks, varied layout, poor consistency, and forgetting the audience.

The result? Clutter, confusion, and distraction.

EEK... LAYOUT IS RANDOM FROM SLIDE TO SLIDE

If you have created an audience-centered template and then copied it to create a canvas for your slides, you should have one look. Yet even then, some things will still create a disconnect. To avoid this, K.I.S.S. (keep it simple students... yeah, that last word can have many interpretations):

- use the same location/layout for headers, bullets, textboxes, and other text
- do not have images with multiple looks (e.g., some are black and white with a 1950's motif while others are neon colors with various geometric shapes)
- keep your font type and sizes consistent between slides

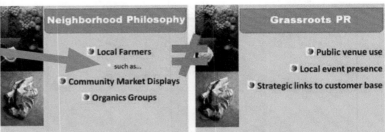

EEK... VISUAL USE OF BULLET *TYPE* DOES NOT MAKE LOGICAL SENSE

When you first learned to write an outline, your teachers schooled you on "levels." They told you that each level or argument rank should be represented with the same level of Roman Numeral or same type of lettering. In a Word document, you may be familiar with outlining options.

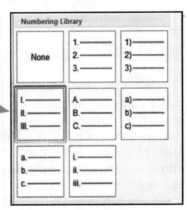

Unfortunately, when you select to bullet a list in PowerPoint, your "outline" is given the same bullets throughout (i.e., A, A, A, A, or II, II, II, II, II). That doesn't make much logical sense. It's up to you to make adjustments to your slides so that the levels of arguments are both clear and consistent throughout your talk.

Be consistent <u>across all slides in your presentation</u>. But DO NOT keep the same bullet type PER LEVEL or just change font size. Here some examples of "Bullet Confusion":

(ALL Apples)

(ALL Dots)

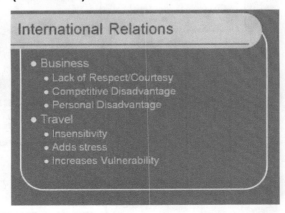

Remember to change the size of bullets *per level*.

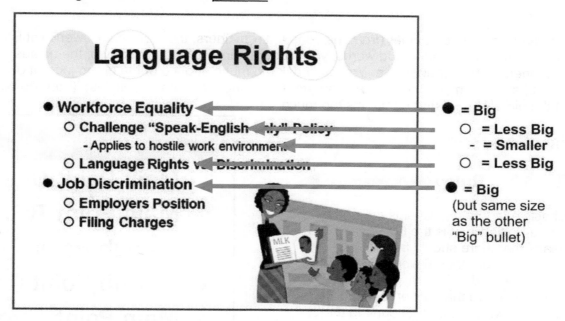

(yeah, yeah... the template has no audience and it is a horrible slide. Good catch! This is just an example of levels.) ☺

As you can see, creating audience-centered templates and keeping the layout of the slide consistent with the verbal outline are the two most basic and crucial elements of slide creation. Sadly, they are often the two most ignored elements of PowerPoint slides. Once you have this big picture mastered, it is time to layer on the other building blocks of your slides in order to finish you slide creation.

TEXTING, TEXTING, TEXTING

Many critics of PowerPoint "how-to" books note the oddity of explaining how to use text on slides *before* discussing visuals when, in fact, PowerPoint is a *visual medium*. Touché! This is a fantastic point – especially when some PowerPoint slides may contain no text at all. The answer to questions of organization is this:

> **Speeches should come before visual aids.** Visual aids... aid. As such, the written work is already done. If you decide, therefore, to use text – you would clarify your ideas by placing the text in your slides *before* placing your visuals. If you choose *not* to use text, it is because you are replacing or *representing* text WITH visuals. An initial discussion of organization, followed by discussions of text and then images keeps the slide logos, purpose, and construction process clear.

If you make a decision to use text on your slides, you must follow two basic rules:
1. **Be Simple**
2. **Be Clear and Legible**

Be Simple

You may vaguely remember (from the constant reminders, thus far) that PowerPoint is a visual medium. If you choose to add words, you must remember that too many of them causes a big disconnect with your audience. You can't ask too much at once of the group in front of you. If you put a book on your slides then you are asking them to read (the slides), listen (to you), look (at the pictures), …. and retain. It's too much.

Not Too Much Text

The 6 X 6 Rule

A basic rule from visual aids created long before PowerPoint is the 6 X 6 rule. This means that there should be:
- no more than 6 words Across a line and
- no more than 6 words that go Down a slide (not counting the header)

For example, this slide has very limited text: *5 words Down and 3 words Across*

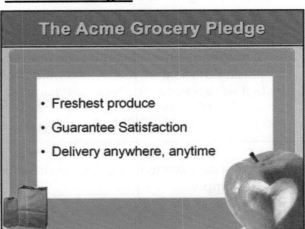

PowerPoint New Math

If you are doing a quick calculation in your head then you have likely realized that 6 X 6 = 36. Ah ha….in PowerPoint we do the "new math." If you were to create a slide with 36 words then you would have a pretty dang overwhelming slide. Too much for your audiences. Instead, practice **no more than 25 words on a slide**. Now that's manageable!

See how editing can help get your audience to quickly grab the information and get right back to you! (Your slides *do not need to be full sentences from your notes*. Edit a bit and keep to key words.) Remember that these aid your talk but the focus should stay on you.

Too Many Words

The Acme Grocery Pledge

- We promise to offer you only the freshest produce available from any grocer
- We unconditionally guarantee your complete and total satisfaction
- We will deliver your groceries to you anywhere, anytime

Ah – Just Right

The Acme Grocery Pledge

- Freshest produce
- Guarantee Satisfaction
- Delivery anywhere, anytime

AVOID TOO MUCH ANIMATION

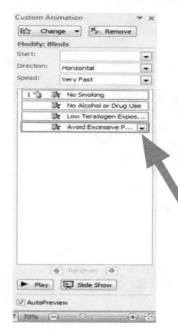

Just like too many words will make your audiences panic, too much animation might make them run for the hills. Animation is the act of bringing in your text either line-by-line or word by word rather than all at once as you show each slide (not to be confused with transitions, which are how you move between slides). Some animation can be a great way to keep your audience's attention on the exact thing that you are saying – too much can make them, well, giggle.

The easiest way to animate is to:
1. Select the text that you want to animate
2. Choose the "Animations" Tab
3. Select Custom Animation
4. Choose Add Effect (and select Entrance, Exit, or Emphasis, as appropriate)
5. Bring in by levels by selecting the arrow down key and Selecting to "Start On Click" for each Level/ Bullet.

Some options for avoiding distractions are:

Avoid Too Many Types of Animation

Each time you change things up on your audience, they take time to adjust. That's time away from listening to you. Each new animation or switch between types takes adjustment (even just a moment or two). Don't give audiences anything to draw their attention away. Select one or **_maybe_** two ways to bring in text and visual elements. (e.g., a _Blinds_ for bringing in text and a _Dissolve_ for bring in pictures but nothing else).

Do Some Grouping

Consider bringing in more than one line of text at a time or with other elements such as photos or images (i.e., remember to stay in sync with your talk – only bring in _as_ you talk about them).

1. Click on one element, then hit shift, and click on a second (or multiple other) elements while still holding shift

2. Right click while "in" one of the elements to bring in the format window

3. Select "Group"
Now you have "one" element with which to contend!!

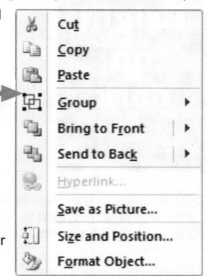

Select Simple Animations

- o some older animations (e.g., Fly, Appear) are overdone and bore

- o some animations take too long (e.g., Diamond, Faded Swivel, Swivel, etc.)

- o some animations are WAY WAY showy, which is another word for annoying (e.g., Pinwheel, Swish, Spinner, etc.)

Some simple animations are Blinds and Dissolve. Try these. They may work for you but if not, think of animation this way… simple. Focus on the talk – not the "show."

WordArt…whew!

If showy animation is too much – WordArt is showy text. Like animation, it might be used for a particular purpose (oh, so rarely) but as a rule, it is always best to avoid using something that grabs more attention than your presentation – or something that in many forms has trouble keeping professional appeal. WordArt can be difficult to re: your audience will spend too much time processing the "art" rather than listening to you!

Be Clear and Be Legible

PowerPoint is, yes, a medium that requires simplicity but also one that absolutely necessitates clarity. If your words cannot be read… then why have them?? It is this need for clarity that lends itself to the following:

Have Strong Contrast

Contrast is the difference in color between your text and your background color. If they are too close in quality then audiences will spend time trying to decipher them rather than quickly reading and getting back to you. Thus, you must have strong contrast.

For example:

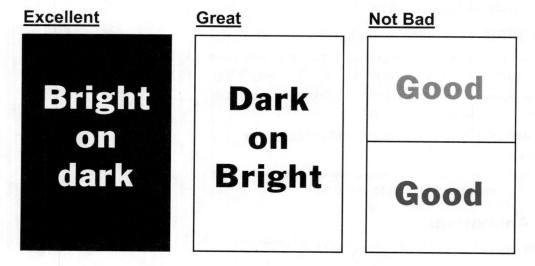

Contrast such as these will ensure that your audience can quickly read every word. Your combinations do not need to be black and white (in fact, other colors can be more visually appealing) but do not sacrifice clarity for pretty colors! ☺

Things to be careful of

Some backgrounds will make text very difficult to see. Watch out for fades (text will be visible on one part of your slide and not another); low contrast (the text is too closely related in color to the background), or… you will have good contrast but the look will be, er, ugly.

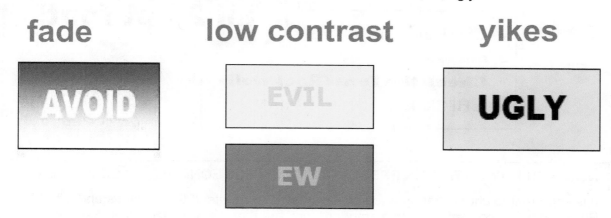

MAKE IT VISIBLE

Sometimes even the best contrast doesn't matter if it is too tiny to see. As you are placing your text (this includes the text on your graphs, charts, or images), think about what can be seen quickly. If you are unsure, print out your slides in full-page version and place them on the floor. Then set a slide at your feet and take **one GIANT step backward**.

Can you still see even the smallest text *easily*?

If not, bump up those sizes. You don't have to go ginormous, just visible.

Stick to:

- Titles (**44** points or bigger)
- Subtitles/ Subpoints (**32** points or bigger)
- Details (**28** points or bigger)
- never <u>below 24 points</u>… even on charts because we *really* need to see those!!

As you adjust your sizes, remember to be consistent across all of your slides. One of the failings of slide creation is when folks adjust their text sizes so that they are more easily seen – but if a phrase doesn't fit… they shrink the size! Everything begins to look random and unorganized.

Consistency is key!

If you need to change your font, (e.g., Arial to Lily to Rockwell to Trajan even if each is in a 32 point size) remember that the size of the words will change. What may be medium size in one font could be **HUGE** or **tiny** in another font. Double check.

> - Check the Font (Arial)
> - **Check the Font (Lily)**
> - **Check the Font (Rockwell)**
> - CHECK THE FONT (TRAJAN)

all 24 pt font!

Note: YOU MAY GIVE YOUR PRESENTATION ON SOMEONE ELSE'S COMPUTER!

It is important to check that other computers have your fonts. If they aren't standard, PowerPoint will convert them to a standard font and then all your sizing will likely be off – even off your slide! Yet, another good reason to stick to basic fonts.

SERIF AND SANS SERIF – AND OTHER "FONTY" DECISIONS

As you are selecting your fonts, remember that some fonts are meant to be read quickly and others take more time to process. Serif versus Sans Serif font choices will greatly help your clarity. Serifs are those little feet or hanging chads at the end of each stroke. Sans means *without* (in French! Use it often to sound very elegant!) and refers to a font without those little feet. See the examples in the box: (Sans Serif) Arial, Tahoma, Lily, Papyrus / (Serif) Times New Roman, Garamond, Bernard, Rosewood.

Serif font faces take a bit more time to read (like in books!) versus Sans Serif, which can be understood with more of a quick glance (quick! Glance at a street sign... what font is that??? Answer: Arial!! No feet!)

Even if you find fabulous Serif fonts or the audience uses these on a website – choose carefully. Some fonts are easier to read and some are sorta hard to grasp. Choose wisely.

Sans Serif
- The quick brown fox jumps over the lazy dog
- The quick brown fox jumps over the lazy dog
- The quick brown fox jumps over the lazy dog
- The quick brown fox jumps over the lazy dog

- The quick brown fox jumps over the lazy dog
- The quick brown fox jumps over the lazy dog
- **The quick brown fox jumps over the lazy dog**
- THE QUICK BROWN FOX JUMPS OVER THE LAZY DOG

Serif

Consider keeping the visual elements and overall feel of your audience's website or public materials but altering font choices for the majority of your slide text for visual clarity.

Header Talk

Headers are like billboards. They can grab attention or fade into the background – they can clarify or confuse. As noted above, headers that reference "subpoints" or evidence are not appropriate visual cues. Once you have the right text, however, what do you do with it?

DON'T SHOUT! Whether in an email from your friend or a slide presentation, "All caps" will have your audience feel like you are yelling (try not to yell at your audience). Sentence case (capitalizing the first letter of the first word) or capitalizing each word in your header are more inviting formats.

In addition, you may consider asking a question. Questions are fantastic means of engaging your audience – but must be strategically employed. Do these match your presentation? Your argument outline? Be sure to clarify your <u>arguments</u> before making stylistic choices!

NO ORPHANED TEXT

Alas, the last and nearly forgotten element to consider with text is orphans. Orphans are, well, small abandoned children. Orphaned text (a term common in graphic design) refers to *abandoned words.*

These are words that are part of a line of text but, due to the length of the line/ sentence, have dropped on to the next line all by themselves. See that poor "orphans" word on the second line? It is all alone in the world. Sad. Edit that sentence to put it closer to its friend words! ☺

Since folks tend to read down a slide, a word alone will take on an individual meaning and be confusing. In addition, words on a line alone take up space to create an awkward layout for the slide with lots of "dead" space.

BAD

GOOD (see? same idea, rephrased!)

Note: Orphaned text does not refer to lists. We get it. They are meant to be read down and not across. Just be careful what you leave "alone."

PROOFREADING

Now that you have finished creating your text, this last step may be the most important. Proofreading. Yes, you know that you should do it and try to be watchful as you are working through your slides. Yet too often bypassing this final check leads to the dreaded…. typo.

Give your text another go round. Did you say "to" when you meant "too"; did you write "weird" when you meant "wired"; did you leave out the one word that allows everything else make sense, or put an extra space between two words? One last check won't hurt you but not doing it just might.

IMAGES, PICTURES, PHOTOS, AND ART (OH MY!)

We have finally come to the most important part of your slides – the images. Why (if this is so important) is it buried in the middle of this book? Well, the organization HAD to come first – we talked about this! Imagine if you just put a whole bunch of cool pictures up and showed them. People might think, "cool," but they would also think… "and, why am I seeing these?" Your organization gives your images a point and an order. Now you must determine what images to use and how to use them.

FINDING IMAGES

So, we spent some time talking about not stealing (that still applies). You may now be a little baffled about where the heck to get pictures to use for your slides, especially audience-centered images. Do not fret. There is a plethora of places willing to give and to sell you pictures.

As you know, if you are in a classroom, your image use *likely* falls under "Fair Use" protection (at least to a certain extent). Once you leave that setting, however, you may not be able to show your slides to anyone but those who own the images. This sorta defeats the purpose of having some great presentations in your portfolio.

Best to start with legally obtained images ready for use in the long run!

INTERNET

Audience Owned/Linked

If you have permission, then your very best place to find images is from your audience. Go to their website (make sure that they have not purchased images that they do not have the right to give you permission to use… you don't want the photographer hunting you down!), search the internet for images of their events, their logos, and their people. Use those as examples for your talk. This is sure to get the "oh… that's us! That's me!" response to your presentation. Your audience will be totally tuned in. Just remember – permission.

Free Online

If you do not have permission from your audience, then you may wish to turn to the ole "world wide web." This vast space is full of free images put up just for public use. Literally, type the phrase "free images" into any search engine to locate several MILLION websites. For example, http://www.flickr.com/creativecommons/ has millions of photos listed by the type of use allowed (i.e., attribution, noncommercial, no derivative works, or share alike. Descriptions of what each label means are on the Flckr website).

Purchased

Many of the free images that you will find have been used by some several thousand folks (after all, they're free). If you would like to look a bit less like the pack, you may consider purchasing some images. Again, some several thousand other folks have done this before you so even in this mode, you must selec your images to do the best that you can to link to the particular audience sitting in front of you.

MICROSOFT POWERPONT

If you have PowerPoint on your computer, you have access to <u>countless images</u>. The software includes a "Clip Art" insertion (w will talk about the merits and definition of Clip Art later in this section) under the "Insert" Tab tht can be searched through for specific images.

CD BOOKS

Any bookseller can offer you an overabundare of books with accompanying CDs that are full of stock images for your use. You can access ard copies of these texts or find online/downloadable versions of image collections.

For instance, simply type in "stock image cd" wh searching on Amazon.com (or other book retailer) and you will find pages of book offerings from general collections to limited compilations of cat images or German houses.

The breadth or depth of your selection is completely up to you. Once you purchase these, they belong to you and you can use them how you see fit.

YOU!!!

Too often, we forget that we are our own best resource. Does anyone not own a camera these days? (If you're wondering, check your cell phone, too! ☺). If you don't take photos, surely your friends have been sending you images of their trips, parties, pets, and activities for quite some time. Start saving them.
Not all of them. ➤

Have a file on your computer where you save the photos that make you laugh or think or could represent something very specific. Save the ones that are beautifully composed. (Be sure to get permission to use these – and, even more so, be professional and ethical in your use.)

You, too, should start to take or save your own images. You can do anything that you want with these: manipulate the color, crop off the sides, distort, change the brightness or contrast, or even combine pictures for a whole new look. This can all be done right in PowerPoint and is totally free.

Note: MAC vs. PC

YOU MAY GIVE YOUR PRESENTATION ON SOMEONE ELSE'S COMPUTER! While you have read this warning for other elements earlier in this book, it is especially crucial to know how to copy, paste, and save images if you are going from MAC to PC.

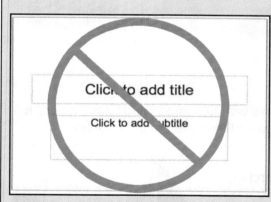

You cannot drag images!! This is a great tool for MAC users but when we switch to a PC, these images come up as empty space holders. Rather than drag, be sure to copy and paste your images so that they may be shown on any type of computer or use the "insert image" function from the images tab.

Some PC to MAC conversions will not work when you have used a Microsoft template that shows pictures. To avoid this, be sure to use a blank slide (no auto-insert boxes) and avoid use of the master slide. Follow the guidelines from above to create a side and then copy and paste it for use as a template.

HIGH QUALITY

Once you have your images, check see if they are of high quality. Yes, this is somewhat subjective. That being said, most of will agree when something is crummy quality – so here are some guidelines to avoid the con:

PIXELS (300x300)

Choose high resolution images. If you select an image online, look at the numbers below it. These will tell you the title, pixels, file size, type of file, and source. Stick to 300 on either side of the "x" to help ensure crisp images.

(Oh… even a large resolution photo not well taken will be fuzzy. Double check how it looks.)

TOO BIG AND TOO SMALL

Yes, size matters – in PowerPoint. If your audience can't see your images because they are too tiny or you have inserted a low pixel image and just stretched it out to make it bigger (and, thus, really fuzzy), well, it matters.

Title

File Size
Type of File
Pixels
Source

... **dog** days of summer – New York Times
1600 x 1200 - 316k - jpg
www.nytimes.com

See what happens when a clear *little* image is stretched big?? He becomes fuzzy! Choose high resolution images and size them to allow them to be clearly seen from the distance of your furthest audience member (typically at least 1/5 of the slide area, which does mean that you must limit the number of pictures per slide).

Big Fuzzy   **Tiny Crisp**

CLIP ART IS EVIL

Many, many, many (ok, most) PowerPoint books will tell you to embrace Clip Art. It is certainly good to feel the love but all images ought to be used thoughtfully. Only a few paragraphs above, you learned of the Clip Art options. If it had no merits, it would not be discussed. So… let's define Clip Art. What PowerPoint has come to offer in this option has changed dramatically since its inception. In early versions, we were treated to classic works such as:

a pointy... "man"??

a "scene" (never sure of what they are, but Microsoft designers seem to love these computer renderings of *thematic events*)

a car (perhaps an early version Ferrari or the new Camero hybrid)

money (or robbing a bank – or, could be someone picking up after their dog with an environmentally friendly bag)

These funky representations of who knows what are traditional Clip Art. They are unclear computer-generated pictures. **Clip Art IS evil.** While your audience is wondering both what and why, you will have lost their attention. Now, we should give credit to Microsoft for updating their image offerings. Today when you click on the same button, you have the option to choose actual pictures but you still have many of these odd creatures. You HAVE options – select what needs no interpretation and grabs!

 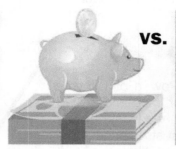 

GRAPHING IT OUT

A good explanatory element can be a well-used graph or chart. You might find that a pie chart helps to show distribution or a line graph clarifies changes over time. The best thing about charts is that they are images that *you create*. As you are determining what chart to put in (and, no, they are not always necessary and can become far more confusing than helpful), be sure to use the best chart in the most illuminating way.

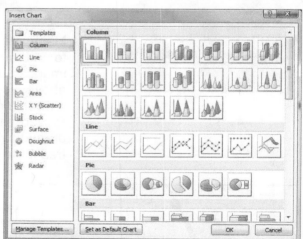

The easiest way to create a chart is to:
1. Select the slide where you want to show your graph/chart

2. Choose the "Insert" Tab and click on "Chart" to bring up the options

   - A blank chart will pop up along with a spreadsheet to complete

3. Fill in data on the spreadsheet... watch the chart change before your very eyes!!

If you have not used a chart before and are not sure what elements to put in which spreadsheet cells, play with it. The image will immediately change to show what you type.

Once you have your information in the chart or graph, you likely will want to alter its appearance for a bit of visual appeal. Right clicking (MAC folks – remember the control key) on the element, such as the font or a particular graph part, will bring up a floating window with format options. Have some fun... but keep your mind on what is helpful rather than what is just fun to create.

EASY!!

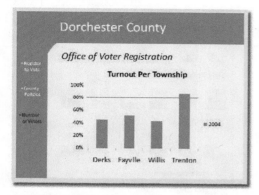

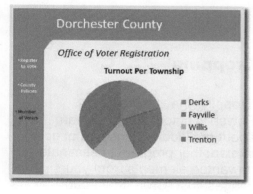

FUN!

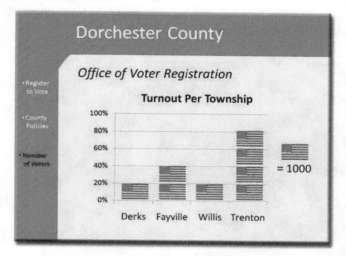

Note: You may be tempted to simply insert another person's chart as an image on your slide. Be sure to follow the guidelines for legally using other's data and images – and, just like with your own graph or chart – alter the text to make it visible to your audience.

(If your copied chart or graph has 13 point font… no one can read it and it will both pull attention away from your talk and diminish the usefulness of the graph itself! Crop out the small text or use a color square to cover the words so that you can re-create them in BIG, VISIBLE sizes!)

ALTERATIONS

Finding pictures is likely not the end of your slide creation story. The pictures that you find may not be in the shape that you want them to be or they could use a bit of enhancement to really grab the audience.

THE "FORMAT" TAB

Only when you select a picture will the "Format" Tab open up in PowerPoint (MAC users will select the image and then open the "Toolbox.") Once it does - it opens up an infinite world of possibilities for manipulating pictures and images. It is likely that you will not use all of those options but there are some basic formatting elements that can help really make images grab your audience.

Recolor

Sometimes what will best make your point is not a picture that you find but one that you create. Altering the smallest details of your picture can have a phenomenal impact! (Just select the "Recolor" option.)

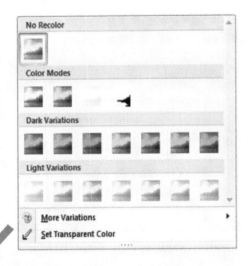

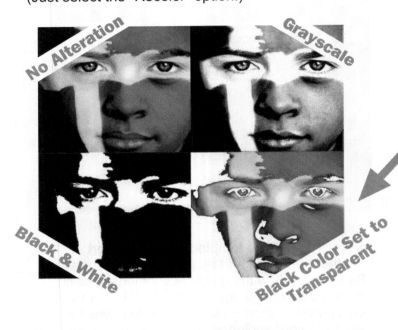

Cropping

Cropping may be the best PowerPoint tool you ever learn about (no kidding)! Instead of going into another program to eliminate unwanted elements from your images, just "Crop" them out.

Now this won't allow you to cut around irregular shapes – it only cuts off the sides but this will make a huge difference in what images you may elect to utilize.

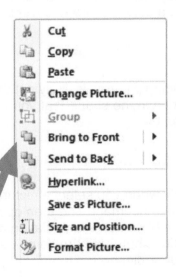

Ordering and Grouping

It is likely that you will have more than one element on your slides. If your pasting does not leave you with the layering effect that you desire, try ordering your elements. Just click on the one that you want your audience to see on top – or put in back – and right click. You will be presented with options to "Bring (the image) to Front" or "Send to Back." MAC users will control click and go to "Arrange."

If you find that you would like to bring in more than one image at the same time, *group* them! Just as was mentioned above in the discussion on animation, one option for bringing items in together is to simply to click on one image, hold the shift key, and click on the next image. While all are still selected, right click to choose Group (MAC users hit click and control.)

Group as many images together as ya like! Now you have <u>one</u> item to move, animate, etc!

To Frame or Not to Frame...

You may elect to "frame" or put a border around your image. This is a very easy step in the "Format" Tab of PowerPoint (select "Picture Border" and choose a line color and weight.) Why?

Well, consider this. If you took a photo, came home, and taped it to the wall, it might be easy for people to see but would it actually draw attention to the image – in a good way? What if instead you popped up to Targét (that's French for the big superstore) and purchased a picture frame for that photo? The entire look of the photo would change and people would be drawn to it in a completely different way. Image frames do the same.

After you have framed your image, you might also want to click on the drop down arrow next to "Picture Effects" and opt for a bit of a shadow (as shown here) for some extra pop!

Framing Irregular Images

The images here are rectangular. If they were irregular then a frame might look, well,… odd. See? Only frame the images that would naturally need a frame!

Note: Keep it simple. <u>The frame should not be what people notice</u> (consider a subtle 1/2 point frame in a grey color – or a color that compliments the photo). However, if you do choose to use a frame, do so consistently with all the photos in your slides. Remember that every change takes time for the audience to adjust.

Nice!

Odd...

DRAG FROM THE EDGES

Once you have your image and it's just lovely, it may need some resizing (make it bigger or smaller). One of the classic new users errors is to try to resize an image by first dragging it from the top and then from the bottom. Guess what? Distorted image! Instead, drag from the corners and the sizing will adjust with you!

Dragged from the sides. (Whoops. Fat dog).

PLACEMENT

Finding pictures is likely not the end of your slide creation story. Where do you put them? As noted above, images should take up at least ⅕ of your slide. Think about where on your slide you will put your elements so that the information is clear.

Think of slides like a billboard that drivers will pass quickly on the freeway. If the layout is simple with a fair bit of room on the slide, then those that speed by will be able to grasp your point quickly. Too much on your billboard or oddly placed??? Well, likely drivers will look away.

Too Much

Less Stuff/Better Placement

NO TEXT / LIMITED TEXT

It is very possible that your slides will have no text at all. WHAT??? No text? Don't all slides have text? They do not. As previously noted, PowerPoint is a visual medium and may simply be the means to *literally* illustrating your point. It is important, however, that you do not simply throw pictures up for the sake of having pictures. Using PowerPoint as a solely visual medium still means that you should follow these four guidelines:

1. Follow the verbal outline
2. Be organized
3. Be clear
4. Stay with the theme

The best means of seeing how to make slides that do not use text (or have limited text) is to *see* your options!

Slides with Main Point Titles and Images (no main point text)

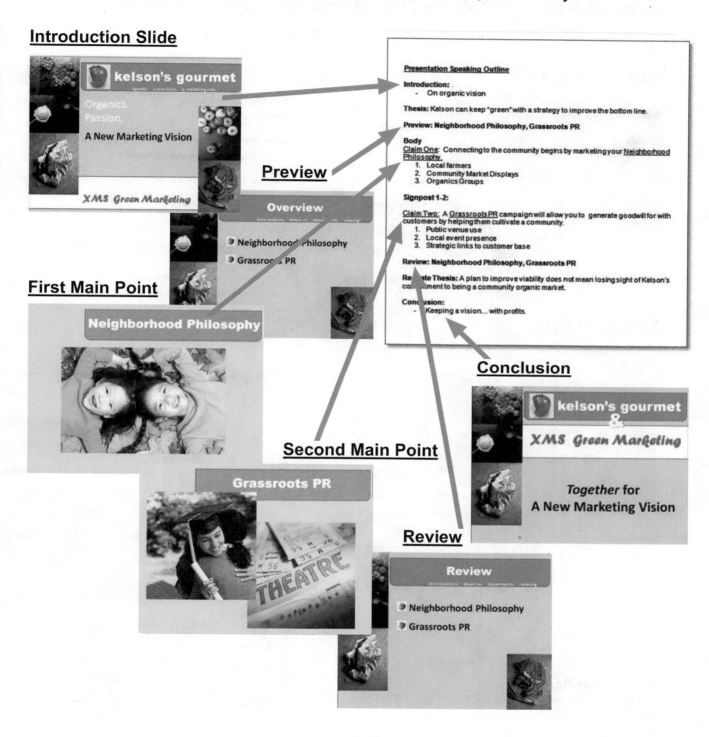

Slides with Images Only for Main Points (no main point text)

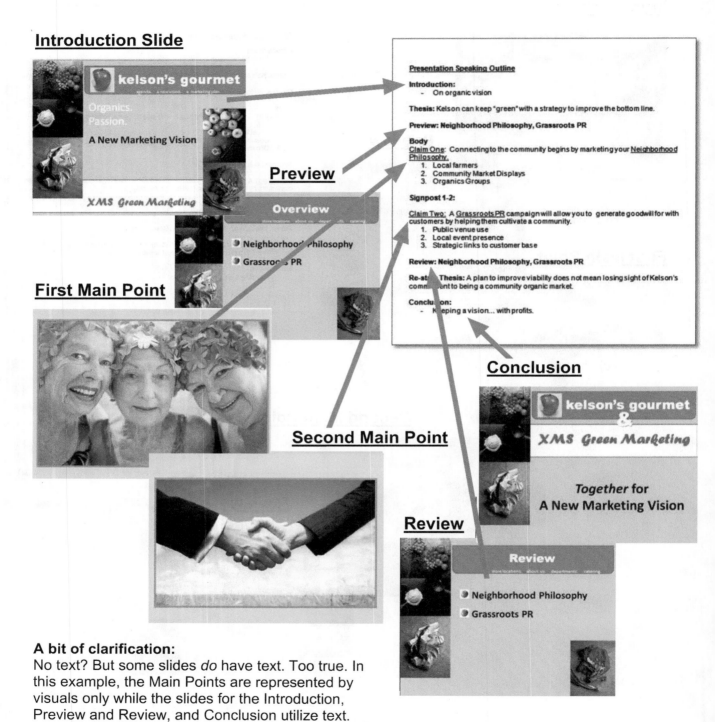

Introduction Slide

Preview

First Main Point

Conclusion

Second Main Point

Review

A bit of clarification:
No text? But some slides *do* have text. Too true. In this example, the Main Points are represented by visuals only while the slides for the Introduction, Preview and Review, and Conclusion utilize text.
The text slides could be eliminated OR be represented by images alone as long as the visual still matches the verbal outline. These slides were left in this version to emphasize that point! ☺

Slides with Images for Main Points and Subpoints / No Text

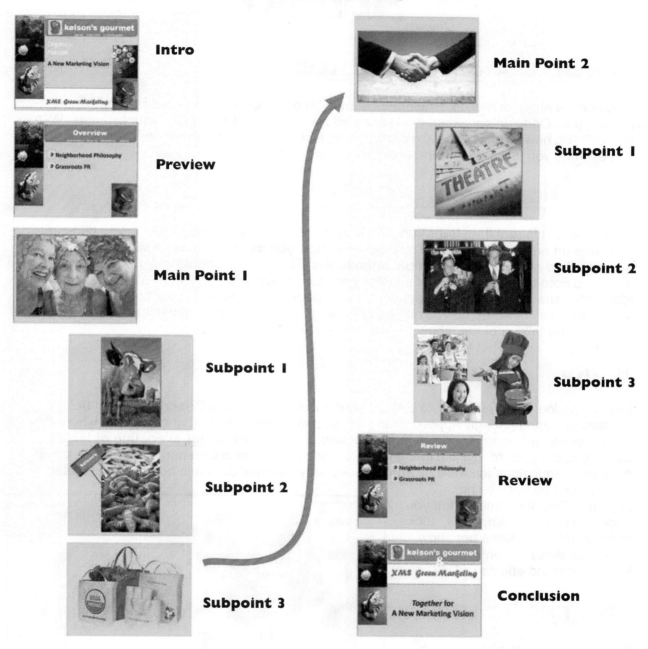

As you can see from the layout represented here, while the slides now contain only visuals (other than the intro and ending slides)… each is clearly linked to the verbal outline and the organization is still evident! Although what you see in these examples are not your only options, they should give you an idea of how to move forward. PowerPoint slides can include moderated text, limited text, or even no text as long as you remember what it is that you are supporting.

And now, you are ready for some bells and whistles!

ADDING

THE BELLS AND THE WHISTLES

This book is about audience. Presenters should be doing everything possible to pull the audience in. Often, in speaking, this means adding a whole lot to capture your listeners. With PowerPoint, however, it typically means adding just a wee bit. Remember to keep the focus on you even as you jazz up your presentation visuals.

ANIMATION AND TRANSITIONS

Animation is different than transitions. Animation refers to the means by which you bring in elements on an individual slide. Transitions are how you move in-between slides. The section on text talked about selecting **simple animations**. This section should only remind you of that edict and note that the concept of simplicity applies to how you move from one slide to the next, too. Slides should generally just appear (no transitions, especially for your first slide, which serves as your backdrop as you begin). Otherwise, keep your choices basic and consistent. Focus on the talk – not the "show."

SOUND

Like animation, in an effort not to distract your audience, sound in PowerPoint must be strategically and sparingly applied. Many of us have sat in a meeting or classroom where the presenter has just learned how to include sound and has done so **for every line of text** or, worse yet, every word. It's like going to the circus!! First there are cameras, then there are drum rolls, then explosions followed by applause – oh my! Audiences would be better captivated if they weren't so busy being appalled. Turn the sound off. If you decide to use it for emphasis, stick to once or maybe twice per show (NOT per slide) is plenty. Better to leave the sound effects to THX.

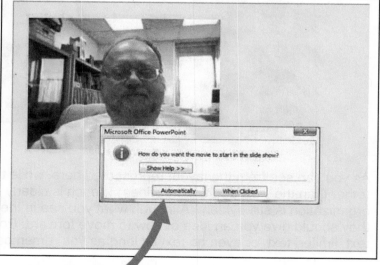

INSERTING VIDEO

Inserting a video is a simple task and somehow always impresses. It is sooooooo easy.

1. Go to the slide where you want the video.
2. Click on the "Insert" Tab
3. Click on Movie
4. Select the Video/ Movie from wherever you have saved it on your computer
5. It will insert and ask....

AutoPlay

It is such an amazing idea that as we talk, our slides will simply advance behind us without our help. It's like magic!! Well, magic may have its drawbacks. Consider that when you have your slides or even your bullets animate and transition automatically, you are positive that you will not alter your speech in any way. You will not take an extra breath, elaborate a little less, or… interact with your audience. These things cannot happen if the slides behind you are moving along on their own. Sometimes just doing it ourselves *is* better.

Unexpected Extras

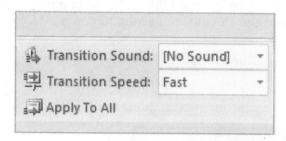

Something else that comes on its own is *embedded* sounds and animation. When you are copying Clip Art from Microsoft or off the internet, be aware that some images will have these extras. You cannot see the auto-animation until the presentation is in the slide show and on the particular slide (i.e., nothing like having your picture start waving to the audience from behind you while you rattle on unaware).

Therefore, it is vital that you run through your presentation with the speakers ON! Who knows what gems you missed during your silent run-through???

Tooooo Much

File Size

You have learned quite a bit. In fact, too much if you applied every trick. The result would be a monstrous file size. The larger your file size, the slower the show will run during your presentation. If you have seen a presenter hit the space bar to advance slides time and time again and nothing happened, then suddenly the slides shot ahead. The file was too large and the processor was catching up.

Your first option for having a smaller slide show file is to include less on it (less pictures, less animations, *no* movies, etc). Option Two is to compress your pictures.

1. Select a picture
2. Choose the "Format" Tab
3. Click on "Compress Picture"
4. Choose to compress just the one you have selected or all the pictures in your slide show.

(**Note**: Sometimes you will get all the benefits of a smaller file and not visibly see any difference in the picture quality. Other times, the pictures will lose some of their crispness. Save your entire presentation first in one location and then compress a second copy of your original. This will save you if the images end up looking crummy).

LOOK WHAT I CAN DO!

Once you know how to do tons of stuff with PowerPoint, you may be tempted to do it all. This is a classic "adding" error. Like any new toy, we become eager to play with it and show it off. Unfortunately, this creates the disconnect about which Tufte (the critic we talked about in our first few pages) was so eager to tell us. Too much focus on our PowerPoint slides forces a division between speakers and audiences.

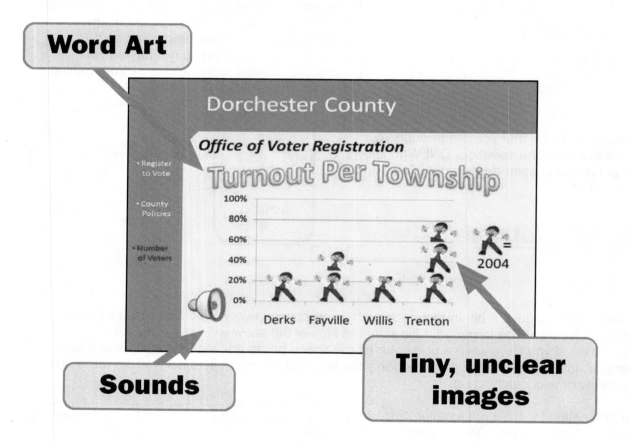

It's an easy fix.

Remember – it's not about you. It's about your audience. Don't show them all your tricks. Show them that you are 100% focused on their needs and that's when they will hang on your every word. Keep it simple.

PRESENTING

DELIVERY

Whoo hoo! Your slides are done! Now what? Well, most PowerPoint books now leave ya hanging. Let's go just a wee bit further (from that communication perspective, again. Don't worry; we won't use the "theory" word). Because your slides are a *part* of your talk, it is crucial that you know how to present them effectively. This includes not allowing them to be the focus of your talk (that's you!) and not allowing them to distract your audience.

INTERACTING WITH YOUR SLIDES

As you begin to practice your presentation (yup – that's a given! Make sure to run through it a few times before actually showing it to an audience), remember that your PowerPoint presentation will give you visual reminders and clarifications of your argument. If you have constructed your slides according to your verbal outline, then you are already in fantastic shape. Now you are in a place to *use* the slides.

Here are some basics:

1. Get the lights right. Be sure to dim or shut off lights prior to starting your talk. PowerPoint presentations are like a romantic date, they need just the right lighting.

2. Know how to get your slide show in presentation mode (er, if you don't know… hit the F5 button to start on slide number 1 or go to the bottom right and click on the screen-looking icon . This will start you on whatever slide you are viewing. MAC users: same button but on the bottom left or ⌘ and return to start from slide 1).

3. Interact with your visuals (talk about what the audience is seeing per slide; look at the slides to make sure that you are not verbally ahead or behind what the audience is following visually. Your audience is looking at those slides… be in sync with them!)

4. Yes, you can touch the screen (point to show your audience what you are talking about – but *avoid* putting your backside to your audience)

5. Don't project on you (get out of the way – let the audience see the slides)

INTERACTING WITH YOUR AUDIENCE

As you know by now, a noteworthy criticism of PowerPoint is that it creates a disconnect between speakers and audiences. It does. In the classroom, you may see students ignore professors while trying to copy every word on every slide without any awareness of the actual lecture. In the boardroom, you regularly can watch eyes glaze over at the beginning of successive slides for sales or department reports.

This is typically because speakers have failed at some of the things that you have already mastered (e.g., being in sync with the verbal, having clear images and organization, etc.). Yet even the most wonderful slide show can disengage an audience. You are a speaker. Be aware of this. Utilize tools that will help keep your audience engaged.

B & W

Learn two amazing buttons that will help focus your audience back on you. The B and W keys allow you to be "in" your presentation but not actually show your slides at that moment.

When your presentation is showing (this won't work in slide sorter or other views), hit B and the screen will go black. To bring it back.... hit the B key again! The same goes for the W key, except that it, obviously, turns the screen white.

Just imagine – you are explaining something and see the audience glaze over. You hit the W key and the room lights up! Now all eyes are back to you. (It's a great trick.) The "B" key works equally as well so that your audience does not see you fumbling to get set up. Go into your room a wee bit early (a good idea anyway to check the set up and become familiar with the setting) and get your slides up and running. Then hit the B key.

When your audience walks in, they see nothing. But when it is time for you to speak, just open your show. No need to show all the slides laid out in slide sorter or giving them a peek at your desktop picture of you at home in your PJs. Instead, just hit the key… and you're on!!

JUMPING SLIDES

Another big criticism of PowerPoint is that it is linear. In other words, some argue that PowerPoint forces the speaker's talk along one path and this path cannot be changed to meet the audience's needs. Pshaw! (That's grandma talk for… nuh uh!!). PowerPoint slides go in the order that you tell them to. Say that you are training a group of sales reps and, as you are about to start, they ask if you can skip to your third point to start. Do not panic! Just do it.

There are many ways to "jump" around in your slide presentation. Most of them involve bringing up a pop up window and clicking on the slide number that you desire. This looks a bit clumsy. Instead, know your slide numbers (bring a print out of all your slides on one page – yes, PowerPoint lets you print like this – or just have a Post-It next to your computer that tells you the slide number where every new discussion point begins. MAC users can cheat a bit. You can use "View Presenter Tools" to see all of your slides while the audience only sees the slide show view). If you know that your third main point begins on slide #24, then once you have finished your introduction simply hit the buttons 2 and 4 and then the Enter key. *Tra la*... you are on slide #24!! (And everyone will just think that you psychically planned your slides just as they would want them).

VIDEO TRANSFERS

Too often folks want to use the captivating elements of a video in their slides but when they go to show it... nothing. There are many reasons that this can happen and a few ways to help to prevent it.

1. Make sure that the computer on which you are showing your slides has the software to show your particular video type (check or ask ahead of time – some video playing software is an easy and free download, but you'll need permission and time).

2. Make sure that the computer can project videos. Sometimes computers and projectors don't like to talk to each other when a video is involved. You may need a tech person with this. However, in an attempt to troubleshoot, try showing only the image from the projector and not viewing it simultaneously on your computer screen. Sometimes this will make them both happy.

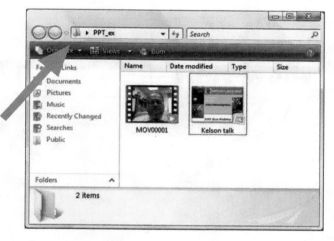

3. Save your video and slide show in a FOLDER and then **copy that *folder*** (rather than the slide show alone) onto the computer that you will use. PowerPoint does not actually put videos into presentations. It puts links into your slide show of where to find the video that you wish to play. Thus, when you get to your video and click on it, the computer looks for it saved in a particular location. If that location is on a different computer... it ain't gonna play. If you have inserted it from this folder and PowerPoint is looking in that folder on the new computer – you're in business!

OOOPS'S

The final steps to presenting your PowerPoint show will prevent some embarrassing mistakes. These blunders make the best stories – but not the best impression.

SCREEN SAVERS

Change your screen saver!!!!!!!!!!!!!!! If you are on a slide in your show long enough for the computer to bring up your screen saver, it will. If your screen saver is pictures of you doing the polka at a family wedding or photos of your last beach vacation, then your entire audience may get to know you just a wee bit too well. Make sure that before each presentation you turn off your screen saver (or, better yet, if you know that you will forget, switch it to something professional and appropriate for public viewing).

STAYING IN PLAY

As you enthusiastically run through your slides, you may find that you run right past your last slide. If you are not familiar with this process, try once at home. What will happen is that you will end up in Slide Sorter view. This shows all your slides to your audience and leaves a rather unprofessional final impression. So, try these quick fixes:

Blank Slides

To make sure that this does not happen at the end of your show, have a "Blank" slide at the end of your show. This slide should be the same background color as all of your other slides (plain white would be jarringly different if your slides all have color and attract attention away from your speech). Be sure that this slide is without any pictures or words. It is not a template… just a background color. This extra slide will ensure that if you do jump ahead, you can keep the audience focused on you.

Hit the Slide Show Button – Again

If you are in the middle of your speech and for some reason pop out into the Slide Sorter or individual slide view – GO BACK!

So many speakers just leave the slides in this awkward viewing format. Don't freak, don't make a big deal about, no need to even comment on it. Just walk over and put the show back in slide show view and go to the appropriate slide. Be calm. ☺

"TALKING" POWERPOINT

Just as much as creating a PowerPoint presentation can enhance or detract from your credibility, so can how you "talk" about PowerPoint. If you inaccurately refer to your presentation then you let your audience know that you have not mastered your work in this medium. To help guide you in your talk, Microsoft (the noble providers of PowerPoint) has provided us with the following simple reminders
(adapted from: http://www.microsoft.com/about/legal/trademarks/ usage/powerpoint.mspx):

"PowerPoint is a trademark that identifies a brand of presentation software from Microsoft." In other words, there are certain legal (but also _accurate_) ways to refer to your presentations!

Incorrect:
- "Send me your powerpoints."
- PowerPoints or Power Points (plural)
- PPT
- PPTs
- Powerpoint

Correct:
- "Send me your PowerPoint slides."
- PowerPoint (singular... this is a proper name and should not be pluralized)

Talk like this will always make you the most erudite individual in the room – and you'll sound smart, too! ☺

A Final Word

It's About Communication

We have reached the end of our journey and, hopefully, PowerPoint now serves a new purpose for you. PowerPoint ought not to fall into the failings of poor visual quality, disconnected audiences, or limited content – not now that we are doing our part in the process of communication.

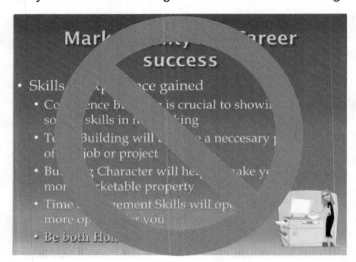

No longer should we be subjected to or ever create slides like these! Instead, by approaching PowerPoint through a new lens, we are able to become more effective and perhaps even help others along the way.

Now you know that PowerPoint is about the audience, to the audience, and *for* the audience. It is about bringing our verbal arguments to a visual place; it is not about us.

Remember what you have learned in these pages. You have:
- a simple means of connecting you to your audience
- step by step instructions for creating <u>audience-centered</u> templates
- tools for altering images *without* the need of other software
- a clear understanding of how slides work *with* your speech
- comfortable delivery techniques that will differentiate you from other presenters
- (of course) a few tricks.

As you continue to craft messages through this medium – have some fun! Play with all that this tool has to offer. As with anything, practice makes better. Your visual messages will improve and the ease with which you create them *will* increase.

NOTES

THINGS TO REMEMBER:

THE LEARNING CURVE

A QUICK TEST

Whether you're in college or not, teaching a class, taking one, or selling the next big thing, it's important to know that the time you spent reading about a new technique has actually taught you something. This section is like the crossword from an in-flight magazine... it's fun to see what you know and *the answers are at the end*!

Have fun!

THINGS TO PONDER

1. The header of each of your slides should always match what other text used on your slides?
_____
_____

 2. What are some common visual outlining errors that, "eek," lead to audience confusion?
_____
_____

3. What are some methods of avoiding distracting animation on PowerPoint slides (no... "don't use animation" is not a correct answer, but nice try! ☺):
_____
_____

4. When you grab images from the internet (legally, of course!) the pixel resolution should be:
_____
_____

5. What is the difference between Serif and Sans Serif fonts AND (yup, this is a two-parter!) which is better for use on your slides (hint: think about what you see while driving)?
_____
_____

6. Why would this sentence undermine your PowerPoint authority?
   * *"I am really proud of my PowerPoints."*
_____
_____

TRUE... OR PERHAPS FALSE

_____ 1. Making "audience-centered" templates in PowerPoint is as easy as changing colors and fonts to mimic the look of your audience's website.

_____ 2. Fair Use guidelines say that we can put whatever we want and as much as we want of others' stuff on our slides as long as we just show them in a classroom!

_____ 3. Once you have a look on your PowerPoint templates that mimics the feel of your audience's website or other public materials (e.g., color and font), you are finished with your design work!

_____ 4. Your first few slides should always state your precise topic and exactly what you want from your audience.

_____ 5. Clip Art is *evil* because it is less professional and open to audience interpretation.

_____ 6. All images in PowerPoint should be "framed" with a simple border.

_____ 7. Cropping images CAN be done in PowerPoint.

_____ 8. All PowerPoint slides must have text.

MULTIPLE GUESS (gosh... it's just like a real classroom test!)

1. Those who don't like PowerPoint tell us not to use it because these slides lead to so much poor communication. You have learned how to design your slides to avoid bad communication elements! What will you avoid?? (hint: there is more than one!)
   _____ a.   Poor Visual Quality
   _____ b.   Audience-Centered Templates
   _____ c.   Disconnecting Speakers and Audiences
   _____ d.   Following a Speaking Outline
   _____ e.   A Preview Slide

2. In both graphic design and for our PowerPoint slides, the term "orphans" is a reference to:
   _____ a.   Small abandoned children
   _____ b.   A slide with only a picture on it
   _____ c.   A word on a line by itself
   _____ d.   New animation for every slide
   _____ e.   B and C

3. If you do it right, then your slides and your speaking outline should always be linked. The best way to make this connection clear is by… (careful: this one is tricky!)
   _____ a.   The look of the slides being linked to the audience
   _____ b.   The headings of each slide matching your verbal preview
   _____ c.   The subpoints on each slide matching the subpoints in your outline
   _____ d.   All of the above
   _____ e.   A and C
   _____ f.   A and B
   _____ g.   B and C

4. Common visual outlining errors that will, "eek," lead to audience confusion include (note: this is another one where you get to select a few!):
   _____ a.   Poor Contrast
   _____ b.   Misleading Headings
   _____ c.   The First Slide Gives It Away
   _____ d.   No Theme for Slides
   _____ e.   Grainy Photos
   _____ f.   The Layout Is Random From Slide to Slide
   _____ g.   Too Much Animation
   _____ h.   Bullet Type Changes Across Outline Levels

5. To make slide text visible to you audience, your font sizes (headers, subpoints, details) should be this size or larger:
   _____ a.   44, 34, 24
   _____ b.   54, 36, 24
   _____ c.   44, 32, 28
   _____ d.   36, 24, 18
   _____ e.   78, 64, 54

6. The maximum number of words that you should have on your PowerPoint slide is:
   _____ a.   44, 32, 28
   _____ b.   54, 36, 24
   _____ c.   36
   _____ d.   25
   _____ e.   24

THE ANSWERS

Let's see how ya did!

THINGS TO PONDER

1. **Answer**: Your preview slide (which comes from the claims of your speech (page 26... and entire outlining section! ☺)

2. **Answer**: (pages 26 – 29)

3. **Answer**: Be Simple (pages 30 – 32)

4. **Answer**: 300 X 300 (page 39)

5. **Answer**: The feet, chads, or lines at the end of each stroke... Serif fonts have them and Sans Serif fonts do not. Sans Serif (without feet) is easier to read on quickly processed visuals such as street signs and, thus, better for your slides. (page 34)

6. **Answer**: PowerPoint is a proper name, it is one word and, therefore, it cannot be made plural. (e.g., "I am really proud my PowerPoint slides." And you should be! You worked hard!!) (page 55).

TRUE... OR PERHAPS FALSE

_____ 1. **Answer**: True (page 11 – 19)

_____ 2. **Answer**: False (page 8, use of images is limited to 10% or 1,000 words)

_____ 3. **Answer**: False (see "note" on page 22, some audience generated materials are not visually pleasing. After creating a mimicked look, you may still need to go back to make edits for visual appeal)

_____ 4. **Answer**: False (page 26)

_____ 5. **Answer**: True (page 39)

_____ 6. **Answer**: False (page 43, do not frame irregularly shaped images)

_____ 7. **Answer**: True (page 42)

_____ 8. **Answer**: False (page 44 – 47,… and throughout).

MULTIPLE GUESS

1. **Answer**: A (page 4), C (page 4)

2. **Answer**: C (page 35)

3. **Answer**: G (pages 25 – 26,… and entire outlining section)

4. **Answer**: B, C, D, F, H (pages 26 – 28)

5. **Answer**: C (page 33)

6. **Answer**: D (page 30)